THE LONELY LIFE WE CHOSE:

Understanding Loneliness and How to Deal with it

Morphy Gold

Table of content

Chapter 1

I could have my friend's company. I had the choice to go out for a movie or hang out with them, go to a party and enjoy life like they do or travel on those trips with them. After all, life is meant to be enjoyed, so I've heard. But I simply can't stand those chit-chats.

 I had the choice to bare my soul to them. I didn't feel I could trust anyone enough to open up. I prefer to be in my own company. I love being in my own company, and enjoy it more than the world and its various distractions. I can say being alone has its benefits.

I love just having to clean when I want to.

I love walking around without clothes on if I want to.

I love watching the shows and movies I want

I enjoy just sitting and reflecting on my simple life

I love reading that book I so crave

I love the silence!!!!

I. Love. Living. Alone.

Outside school hours, I spent much of my childhood home alone and I suppose this had a part in forming my personality. I got quite self-reliant and I missed out on much that is supposedly nice and enjoyable about childhood.

I learned how to do without human companionship, and the down side of that is that I found making friendships extremely hard. I spend too much time in my head, and too little time in the company of others. I have gotten so acclimated to it that I am hesitant of accepting social invites

There are days I simply do not feel like talking to anybody. My friends take it personally that I do not want to spend time with them. I slip out of conversations because my emotional battery is winding down and needs recharging. It's not personal; I just prefer to be alone almost all the time. I don't believe I'm weird; I'm simply not cut out for those painful small talks

One of the most unpleasant things is that I am losing the ability to converse since I get so little conversation. I stumble over words and have to work hard at constructing cohesive phrases - quite unnerving. I find it much simpler to write than to talk. I express myself freely through writing.

If eventually I go out, I only hang out with groups of friends in small appearances which I generally start to regret almost immediately, though, not always.

Now I'm an adult and just feel sometimes awkward with people. Of course, I love socializing and talking to people but the feeling does not last long, after a few hours I will start talking less to others and my mind will zone out and go wander somewhere else

I get sad when people joke that I'm anti-social and dislike humanity only because they cannot conceive a world where everyone is not as outgoing as they are.

I despise small talks and feel trapped by inane questions such as "what did you do over the weekend"

I feel lonely when I'm with a bunch of people and talking about nothing.

I feel nervous when my phone rings or when I have to make a phone call...

These sentences are precisely what I felt!

I feel like I have struggled with some sort of loneliness all of my life.

Some believe that being alone is intolerable, others revel in it. I have been both persons.

I had a lonely life, and I want to be alone for the most part, mostly because when I am with a lot of people I still feel lonely. You can feel lonely even while you're surrounded by other people

While I would say that having alone time is good once in a while; too much loneliness can be detrimental to one's health. Of course, I cherish my lone time, but there are days I resent it, there are days I long for companionship. Everybody likes to feel loved and involved once in a while

You feel alone or empty, and you want to connect with people, but your feelings of loneliness make it difficult to do so.

 You feel hopeless and sometimes resign yourself to living the rest of your life this way.

But loneliness isn't something that you have to manage on your own alone, and while it could be challenging, there are things you can do to feel more connected to those around you. I had to engage in a struggle against loneliness by pushing myself to go out and also volunteer more.

It wasn't easy yeah! Who said it will be easy, but I can say it was worth it.

Though you may not totally recover from extreme loneliness, there are possibilities you may feel lonely from time to time, but you can adopt a lifestyle that helps you to deal with loneliness.

In this book, we'll take a look at what loneliness is, and how it is different from comparable ideas like isolation and solitude. Then will analyze numerous causes and common types of loneliness, as well as the detrimental consequences loneliness may have on our lives. Finally, we will end by addressing ways to deal with loneliness healthily.

About loneliness

If you're reading this, chances are you know what it's like to be lonely. That means you realize that loneliness may sometimes seem like it'll never stop and that you can sometimes be surrounded by friends and family and yet feel shut off from the world.

We all feel lonely from time to time. Feelings of loneliness are personal, thus everyone's experience of loneliness will be distinct.

You may prefer to be alone and live contentedly without much contact with other people, whereas others may find this a lonely experience.

Or you may have lots of social contacts, or be in a relationship or part of a family, and still feel lonely especially if you don't feel understood or cared for by the people around you

When we feel lonely, we often try to beat ourselves up and assume that something is simply wrong with us. The more alone we feel, the more we start to develop ideas of not belonging or of feeling rejected by others. Left alone with our thoughts, we become our own worst adversary.

A secluded environment is the ideal breeding ground for negative, self-critical ideas. These thinking patterns make up the critical inner voice, an internalized adversary that leads to self-destructive thought processes and behaviors. This inner critic feeds into feelings of isolation, prompting us to shun people and stay in a lonely condition.

Although our critical inner voices may tell us differently, in truth, there is nothing innately wrong with us that prompt us to feel lonely. It is a prevalent misperception that individuals feel lonely because they have weak social skills. In reality, a recent study demonstrates that lonely persons have excellent social abilities and even outperform non-lonely individuals when it comes to interpreting social signs.

Loneliness is not characterized by the quantity of time we spend alone, but rather by how we feel about the time we spend alone. Feeling lonely might provoke beliefs that we are unwanted or unlikeable.

Your critical inner voice will come up with a terrible list of reasons why you feel lonely, brutally assaulting you. For example, you may criticize yourself for being awkward or creepy and then as a result act quietly among a gathering of people. You may then criticize yourself for not talking enough. These ideas represent a harsh and antagonistic attitude of view toward oneself.

What is loneliness?

Loneliness has no formal definition. Any definition may not fit with everybody's experience, since I believe it is fair to say that no two people's feelings of loneliness are the same.

It's also vital to at least come up with a workable definition that can be agreed on.

Loneliness is an unpleasant feeling or emotion that stems from a lack of closeness with other people or oneself. It's a subjective term: feeling lonely indicates you are lonely.

In my personal experience, what seems to describe loneliness is the lack of closeness with other people. This lack of intimacy may arise on the physical level, shared interests or beliefs, or emotional level in which the emotional level is the core of it- that is, it's about not feeling well connected with other people on an emotional level.

Most individuals will feel lonely at some time in their life. But if you feel lonely most or all of the time, it may have major detrimental implications on your health and wellness.

Loneliness is frequently associated with elderly people; however, loneliness may be widespread amongst young people as well. Recent research suggests that young people feel loneliness more intensely, and more frequently than any other age group

Loneliness is an internal feeling that originates from perception rather than an outward state of affairs. Loneliness is different from isolation. Many people who are alone suffer loneliness. But many individuals seek out isolation and view it as a positive thing.

When this occurs, we typically characterize it as solitary. It's also worth mentioning that solitude is not a condition for loneliness: you might feel lonely even while you're surrounded by other people. Many individuals experience the most severe spells of loneliness happening exactly when they are surrounded by others.

Loneliness can be painful. But is vital to be clear about this as many people feel the most comfortable when they are alone from others. As we noted above, many individuals seek out isolation because they find it therapeutic or useful in encouraging creativity.

Do we choose loneliness?

I noticed as I began to write about loneliness, how frequently it may affect us every day. Loneliness may start from an early age in the playground for example. We might have noticed, when looking at all the youngsters enjoying fun and playing, that there are definite moments of feeling detached: seeing everyone, but isolated from everyone and feeling rather alone? Sometimes we have that feeling of not belonging there, we just couldn't fit in.

We might have a picture like this of what loneliness looks like, fully established from our earliest days . . surrounded by others but lonely. Is this still occurring in our adult life surrounded by family, friends or work colleagues, but lonely? Lets say you were invited to a party by your friends, and you accepted with the high expectations that perhaps this will be different. On getting there, seeing the different faces and outfits, you feel that feeling of being different or not belonging wash over you and chose to withdraw to yourself once again.

Is it possible that we have a choice as to whether we feel lonely or not? Is it a particular way we choose to be that does not stay open to trusting others and makes us defensive and subsequently, shut down?

Perhaps being lonely is not a symptom of life but a decision within life. Loneliness, I have realized, depends totally on what I choose and how I am feeling when I choose it.

Loneliness and Isolation

While the evidence reveals that loneliness and isolation are unhealthy for both mental and physical health, being alone is not the same as being lonely, although they are associated.

In truth, isolation provides a variety of critical mental health advantages, including helping individuals to better concentrate and rejuvenate.

Loneliness is the sense of being alone or separated, while isolation is the absence of social interactions and having few people to communicate with frequently.

Loneliness is a sensation of undesired isolation or lack of connection, whether you are alone or surrounded by people. Solitude, on the other hand, is a decision. People may choose to stay alone for hours or days and not feel lonely at all

Loneliness is characterized by feelings of solitude while craving social relationships. It is typically regarded as an unintentional separation, rejection, or abandonment by other people.

Solitude, on the other hand, is voluntary. People who love spending time by themselves continue to retain solid social interactions that they may return to when they want connection. They still spend time with other people, but these interactions are tempered by periods spent alone.

Solitude may be a lovely thing unless it goes on too long and slips into loneliness,

Studies have indicated that living alone is a risk factor for loneliness But, research also reveals that time spent alone may aid with feelings of autonomy, self-discovery, and developing a serene attitude,

In other words, being alone may but doesn't necessarily create loneliness.

Due to the COVID-19 epidemic, feelings of isolation and loneliness have intensified, making it tougher for everyone to spend time with others. Older people are at a higher risk of loneliness, but everyone must attempt to keep connected where possible by exploring ways to keep connected such as by meeting up, phone conversations or video chats that may help battle feelings of loneliness.

When do people feel lonely?

Loneliness may hit anyone at any moment. Sometimes you may not even feel lonely for an evident cause, and what you're feeling might always be tied to other problems like sadness or anxiety.

But a lot of individuals indeed tend to feel lonely during important life events. Maybe you're moving house or having a career change in a new city. Maybe you are getting divorced. Maybe you're moving from one school to another. Or maybe you simply feel like your friends are beginning to get into things that don't interest you.

All of these factors might be making you feel lonely and lost, and you could find it hard to connect with others around you.

Why do we feel lonely?

I suppose there's a very large variety of a plausible reason for loneliness. For one person, being molested as a child might be the source of loneliness. For another individual, being in a relationship with someone who has a hard time communicating might be the reason for their loneliness. And for another, a mental habit of negative self-talk might be the root of their loneliness.

It is crucial to remember that loneliness is a considerably more subjective sensation than we think. Whether someone feels lonely depends greatly on their background, personality, culture, living environment, temperament etc.

Because loneliness is so common, it seems logical that there are also lots of various reasons why individuals feel lonely.

Here are a few of the prominent ones:

- *Feeling alienated from friends.*

Ever felt that even if all of your friends are one push of a button away, you're still not truly connected to them? You can struggle with loneliness even while having tons of friends especially if they are surface level friends- people that exist in your periphery with whom you have no deep connection.

You can also feel distant from friends if you hide your true self from them perhaps for the fear of not being accepted for who you really are which creates a strong sense of emotional loneliness even when surrounded by people. Sometimes, emotional distance can also occur when we do not talk about our struggles or how we feel; probably we feel insecure about certain aspects of our life or we have a history of being judged or misunderstood, so we choose to alienate ourselves from others

- *Not Fitting in.*

There are times in our life when we feel like we do not fit in. This could be due to shyness from a young age, career change in a new city or moving into a different cultural dynamic. You may also experience not fitting in when you have different interests from the individuals at your school or workplace. Or maybe you simply dress differently. In any event, feeling like you don't fit in may make the feelings of loneliness even worse, and can mean is much more difficult to meet people and feel connected.

- *Being Single*

Being single can be lonely and this can have real impacts on our lives. According to Aristotle, Man is by nature a social animal. Thus, humans are social and pair oriented by nature, and so it is common for those who are not in relationships to feel lonely some time.

Whether it is your friends all going into relationships and dating, constantly watching dating programs on TV, or feeling pressure from your family to bring someone home, it might seem like romantic connections are at the front of everyone's thoughts. It might be a terrible feeling like you're missing out on something especially when you are single. These feelings can bring about loneliness

- *Social anxiety*

Social anxiety disorder also called social phobia is a specific form of anxiety usually characterized by excessive fear and self-consciousness about daily social interactions where you compulsively worry about others evaluating you or being humiliated, judged or mocked. It can be hard to make close connections and relationships when you feel too anxious around people.

- *Trauma*

Trauma occurs when an especially painful or disturbing events leads to a sustained fear or anxiety response. Living through stressful experiences may raise the risk of posttraumatic stress disorder (PTSD), which may induce panic episodes. For example, people who suffered abuse as a child may develop a prolonged fear of people of the same gender as the person who abused them which may lead to the inability to make genuine connections and being around a lot of people

- *Looking after a parent or sibling.*

Being the main caretaker for someone dear to you who is unwell or has a disability may often make you feel like you weigh the world on your shoulders. For example, for those who have a sibling with Down's syndrome, or a mother with bipolar, being a caregiver might leave you feeling like you can't really speak to others much alone invite them over for dinner or a sleepover.

- *Low Self –Esteem*

You may be hesitant to meet or engage with other people if you have lack confidence in yourself because it makes you think poorly of yourself and also imagine that others think poorly of you as well. Low self-esteem causes you to feel unworthy of other people's time or attention. This can lead to loneliness. The chronic feeling of unworthiness can also prevent you from connecting on a deeper or more intimate level when you are in a relationship or close to others.

- *Mental or physical health issues*

Living with health issues can be isolating. A variety of mental diseases including bipolar, anxiety and depression can also increase the risk for loneliness.

Mental illness might make you apprehensive about meeting people, so you might spend more time inside. Or it might lead to sleeplessness, which in turn can leave you exhausted, irritated and lonely.

- *Disability*

A multitude of impairments may frequently make individuals feel as if there is no one around them who cares. These sentiments may grow considerably worse if people in public are unpleasant or impolite, and confronting everyday prejudice can make loneliness even more difficult to endure.

- *Racism.*

People who confront racism believe that being discriminated against might make them feel alone, and can make it difficult for them to build true friendships. Racism takes a variety of forms, all of them harmful, thus often even a small or casual act of racism may have huge repercussions on someone's self-esteem.

What Does Loneliness Feel Like?

Symptoms of loneliness tend to cause a downward spiral. When you're lonely, you feel sad or rejected. You may also feel like you are lacking something important when you are alone. So you retreat and become more critical of yourself and the people around you. This, however, isolates you more, frequently fostering deeper loneliness

Symptoms of loneliness vary based on what's causing it and the people's specific circumstances. But loneliness generally entails the following

> - Feeling left out or alienated from others
> - A sad feeling, emptiness, or disconnectedness
> - A craving for companionship

➤ Feeling like no one listens to you

➤ Feeling solitary even though you're surrounded by people

➤ Feeling weary or worn out by social encounters

➤ Decreased appetite and incessant crying

➤ Feeling insecure, timid, or introverted when it comes to social interactions

➤ Ruminating and reflecting on the past

More severe symptoms of loneliness might include:

- Insomnia or sleeping more than usual

- Feelings of worthlessness, self-doubt or hopelessness

- Withdrawal from social activities

- A strong desire to miss out on meeting up

Unusual red flags that are also a sign of loneliness include;

- Buying superfluous stuffs out of boredom or to fill a void might be a symptom of loneliness.

- Paranoia or feeling like others are criticizing you
- Loss of appetite or a rise in binge eating or self-soothing with food might both be warning flags

You may detect the signs and symptoms above in yourself or your loved ones going through loneliness. Hence, you must try to make an additional effort to put yourself out there socially, discover strategies to address your lack of connection and ask for help since loneliness may have a big influence on mental health.

How Loneliness Changes Across Lifetime

Loneliness may hit at any age, but the reason could be different. Most individuals experience loneliness at some point throughout their lives, Researchers found that loneliness ebbs and flows as we age, in quite predictable ways. Counter-intuitively, we tend to be lonelier while young and likewise when old. Understanding why we get lonely in particular life phases might enable us to overcome the unsettling emotions of isolation when they inevitably arrive.

Different types of loneliness

There are different types of loneliness including existential, social and emotional loneliness

Loneliness may also be a fleeting experience that comes and goes.

It might be situational; for example only occurring at specific periods like weekends, holidays or Christmas.

Or loneliness can be chronic; this implies someone feels lonely all or most of the time.

Loneliness may also be described by its intensity, or how strongly it is felt, which may change from moment to moment and throughout various periods.

Existential loneliness

Existential loneliness is the result of a wider separation related to the nature of existence and in particular, a lack of meaning in life. An individual may be in the company of others or surrounded by love but still experience existential loneliness

Existential loneliness involves the state of ones own sense of meaning and purpose in the world. For example, it is common for older people to feel their sense of meaning and purpose slip away, especially if they experience a loss of independence.

Existential loneliness is also about the sense of a lack of wholeness, like you feel empty and incomplete and you have no idea what to do about it.

From an existential standpoint, a little amount of existential loneliness is beneficial for the soul, and it is undoubtedly an inherent component of the human experience. However, loneliness tends to bring up unpleasant sentiments, and although it might be beneficial in terms of self-exploration, it is also something we dislike and wish to avoid as much as we can.

Social Loneliness

Social loneliness is the absence of a larger social network of friends, neighbors or coworkers.

This sort of loneliness is experienced by those who have problems in social situations because of low self-esteem, social awkwardness or shyness. This makes them doubt their ability to be entertaining in social circumstances.

You could also suffer social loneliness even while you're in a relationship. If you don't have a larger circle of social support, you may feel that you and your spouse don't have a group with whom you belong. When you go to a party and don't recognize anybody familiar, you may experience a feeling of social loneliness, especially if you don't generally feel comfortable approaching new people.

Emotional Loneliness

Emotional loneliness is the situation of feeling emotionally isolated from the people around you or being unable to connect with them on a deep or meaningful level. For example, the absence of a significant other with whom a meaningful relationship existed which may be a lover or close friend

Emotional loneliness includes feelings of isolation, abandonment and emptiness.

Emotional loneliness originates from a feeling that you lack connections or bonds. You could sense emotional loneliness when everyone except you has a love relationship in your group.

You may also feel emotional loneliness when you need someone to speak to about anything going on in your life, but feel that there is no one available. If your heart has shattered, you could feel lonely for the person who has gone out of your life. You could feel lonely for a close friend, a parent, a sibling etc. If you're feeling this form of loneliness, the perceived poor quality of your connections is driving you to feel this way.

Just like any other type of loneliness, emotional loneliness may be induced by different circumstances.

Some of the most typical triggers include:

- Parental neglect in childhood. Some theories imply that people are more likely to struggle with forming intimate emotional relationships as adults if they didn't experience such attachments with a parent or parent-like figure as infants or children

- Trauma in childhood or adulthood. Trauma that happens throughout childhood or adulthood may also make it difficult for people to build solid connections with others, which may add to feelings of emotional loneliness. The best course of action for victims of trauma who are battling emotional loneliness is to get counseling from a skilled specialist.

- Substance abuse. Studies revealed that people who use substances are more likely to feel emotionally lonely.

- Situational Life Changes: In some circumstances, a person could develop short-term emotional loneliness when a relationship starts to break down or ends in divorce, while migrating to a new place, career change, or confronting other substantial changes in their life. During such transitory situations, loneliness will often resolve with time as a person acclimates to these changes.

It is also important to note that emotional loneliness stands separate from other types of loneliness and it is not the same as emotional isolation.

What Is Emotional Isolation?

Emotional isolation is the act of withdrawing from others on an emotional level.

Emotional isolation can act as a defense mechanism that leads a person to seal oneself off in the company of other people. It is defined by shallow communication and purposeful avoidance of serious, personal relationships or meaningful friendships.

While emotional loneliness is the condition of feeling distant from others (even if you may seek connection), emotional isolation is the act of drawing yourself away from the people around you whether it's deliberate or not.

When utilized as a purposeful defensive technique, emotional isolation is a way of maintaining connection and communication on a surface level to prevent building deep or meaningful connections with others. Sometimes, emotional solitude may be a purposeful decision for someone who has a vast group of acquaintances

A person may use emotional isolation as a barrier to protect themselves from feeling vulnerable or being hurt especially, if they struggle with trusting people.

Emotional isolation may result from trauma and may be an indication of underlying psychiatric disorders.

If emotional isolation is accompanied by feelings of anxiety, despair, or paranoia, then a discussion with a medical expert may be needed.

Chronic loneliness

Chronic loneliness arises when feelings of loneliness and unpleasant social isolation carry on for a lengthy period that it almost becomes a way of life.

Chronic loneliness is characterized by frequent and relentless feelings of being alone or isolated from others, and an inability to connect on a deeper level. It may also be accompanied by deeply seated sentiments of inadequacy, low self-esteem, and self-loathing.

Some people may go through short-term bout of loneliness at some point in their life. These sorts of feelings are often short and not considered chronic. However, when feelings of loneliness and isolation increase and linger long-term, there may be more significant signs to be aware of and things you can do to cope with chronic loneliness

Ongoing loneliness may strike even the most outwardly extroverted individual. Being the "life of the party" doesn't always exempt someone from being chronically lonely. This form of chronic, or long-term loneliness, may ultimately impact all parts of your life.

Primary indications and symptoms of chronic loneliness

Signs and symptoms of chronic loneliness might vary based on who you are and your environment. If you routinely experience any or all of the following, you may be dealing with chronic loneliness:

- No best or close friends. When you have friends, but they are casual friends or acquaintances and you believe you can find no one who really "gets" you.

- The inability to connect with people in a deeper or more personal level. You may have friends and family in your life, but contact with them is at a very superficial level. Your engagement with them doesn't seem linked in a manner that is fulfilling and the gap appears never-ending.

- Unreciprocated attempts to reach out (or connect) or exhaustion while trying. When dealing with chronic loneliness, attempting to connect and be sociable with people might leave you feeling weary, especially when your attempts are not reciprocated and you are not seen or heard. Continued emotions of being depleted may lead to additional concerns including sleep problems, a weaker immune system, poor eating etc.

- The overwhelming feelings of isolation regardless of where you are and who is around. You can be surrounded by dozens of people and, yet, you feel alienated, detached, and disconnected. For example, you may be at work, a party, or on a bus, where you are surrounded by people and still feel alienated and alone. Same when you are strolling along a crowded street. It's as though you're in your indestructible bubble.

- Negative sentiments of self-doubt and self-worth. You may feel like you are constantly less than enough. These feelings, long-term, are another probable indication of chronic loneliness.

Who's most at risk for chronic loneliness?

Chronic, loneliness may affect all sorts of individuals. It's tempting to believe that someone whos usually quiet or introverted could be more in danger, but extroverts can also suffer from chronic loneliness, even if they may seem to be the life of the party. This form of loneliness is not specific to one personality type.

For some individuals, chronic loneliness may become a side effect of a physical or emotional disorder, including those dealing with the following issues:

- Substance usage

- Serious illness or disease

- Depression and bipolar disorder

- Sexual orientation issues etc.

All of these concerns might potentially contribute to long-term feelings of loneliness and isolation.

How Can Loneliness Impact Mental Health?

Frequent and long-term feelings of loneliness may impact your health in various ways. For example, persistent loneliness may push up cortisol levels in the body. Cortisol is a hormone that the body generates while under stress. Over time, elevated cortisol levels may result in inflammation, insulin resistance, excess weight gain, trouble focusing, and more.

Certain mental health conditions may contribute to loneliness, for example, social anxiety (also known as social phobia). People with social anxiety often find it difficult to participate in ordinary activities involving other people, which can lead to a lack of meaningful social interaction and ultimately, feelings of loneliness.

If you identify yourself with an incapacity to connect with others, it might foster negative ideas and sentiments about self-doubt and self-worth. Equally, feeling socially cut off or isolated may damage your opinions of yourself and, in consequence, your mental health

Loneliness can lead to unhealthy and risky behavior due to lack of will power and motivation.

For example some people can feel so low or depressed that they begin to neglect themselves.

Research shows that people who suffer from loneliness or depression tend to eat more junk food because it fills some sort of void or gives a temporary satisfaction. Junk eating is unhealthy and can lead to health concerns such as diabetes and obesity.

Loneliness can also impact peoples health through alcohol and drug misuse. When lonely, some people tend to develop self-destructive habits which may include heavy drinking, experimenting with drugs or using substances to cope with their pain. During these episodes, people may binge, overuse or in some extreme cases overdose on substances

Feelings of loneliness can lead to increased stress in some people which can lead to insomnia. Poor sleeping habits can impact the neural, hormonal and metabolic regulation of our body systems while good sleeping habits can strengthen the immune system.

Symptoms of chronic loneliness, when left unchecked might put you at a greater risk for more serious physical and mental health problems, including: Depressions, high blood pressure, sleep disorders, heart disease, diabetes, substance usage etc.

There is also the chance that prolonged loneliness and the health concerns that come with it, might reduce one's lifespan. If you believe you are dealing with long-term feelings of loneliness, go to your therapist or a medical professional.

Chapter 2

Ways to handle loneliness.

There is no single approach to fight loneliness and while it could be challenging, it doesn't mean that loneliness is impossible to conquer or that you will suffer it forever. Everyone feels lonely at some point in their lives. While this doesn't make the feeling any better, it is encouraging to know that others feel the same as you and there are things you can do to feel more connected to those around you.

Some strategies for dealing with loneliness include:

- *Admit you are lonely*

A first step to conquering loneliness is acknowledging how you feel and the influence it's having on your life. Name it and validate it. Get genuine about what you're going through. Telling other people you're lonely may seem intimidating, embarrassing, and self-defeating, "since there's a lot of stigma around loneliness. But articulating that feeling might be the beginning of releasing it.

Denying our loneliness simply reinforces it, so before we can heal, we have to be honest at least with ourselves about what we are feeling."

- *Recognize you are not alone in that lonely feeling*

If 22 percent of Americans regularly feel lonely, know that you are sharing the same experience with millions of other people. When you are feeling lonely, remind yourself exactly how ubiquitous loneliness is and picture yourself being linked to all of the lonely individuals out there.

- *Practice self-care*

The potential power of exercise, a decent diet, sufficient sleep, sunlight, and even meditation in combatting loneliness cannot be underestimated. Looking after your physical wellness concurrently helps with your emotional wellbeing

A good diet may influence your health, too. A regular diet of sugar, preservatives and overly processed food may have severe effects on your physical and emotional health. Focus on eating complete meals for a time and see if this will assist in your approach to fighting loneliness.

Sleep quality is intimately connected to emotional wellness. Loss of sleep or bad sleep patterns may worsen feelings of loneliness and isolation and vice versa.

If you're battling loneliness, consider adopting healthier sleep habits. Limit sweets and caffeine before night, switch off digital gadgets for some relaxation time and make sure your bedroom is quiet and dark.

- *Take a Walk or spend time with nature*

One of the simplest methods to not feel lonely is to take a walk! Walking, which is both a peaceful and an energetic exercise, is one of the finest methods to stay fit. Walking also helps us maintain our emotional and physical health, particularly while feeling lonely.

Even a thirty-minute walk every day will reduce your heart rate, reduce anxiety, and alleviate stress and it can be quite scenic.

Strolling in nature may be meditative, too, "primarily because we can realize just how much life is out there beyond human existence and how naturally connected we are to it". Take the time to examine the world around you. Get outside, take a walk in the park, or hang out by the water, take some time to listen to the birds. Absorb the sights, sound and smells of nature. Feel the breeze on your face.

- *Joining a class or clubs*

Joining a club and meeting individuals who share the same interest or passion with you is another way on how to deal with loneliness. It's a great way to make friends and get together with like-minded people. This can help you to build deep meaningful relationships or form bonds with other people.

There are various clubs and classes available to join or take part in, such as book clubs, fitness classes, cooking classes and art classes. Many of these groups may be found on the internet or through community organizations.

Go for any activity that puts you in a social environment on a regular basis. You can check your community services to find out what is available around you.

- *Volunteering*

Volunteering is a great opportunity to meet new people while helping a cause you believe in. Often charities and local groups require additional volunteers and it may lead to feelings of gratitude and give you a sense of true purpose knowing you're helping others.

Dedicating a day to helping the elderly or cooking meals at a soup kitchen would meet your urge to feel needed and take you away from the self-centered perspective that loneliness brings on. Also, the time you spend getting to know the people you're helping will bring out some of the closeness and connection you've been yearning for.

- *Strengthening existing ties*

If you already have people in your life such as old acquaintances or family members, it might be good to reach out to them and deepen your connections with them. Organizing to visit them or spending time chatting with them and getting to know them better may help with feelings of loneliness and lead to more encounters in the future.

Try to make a list of the people you haven't seen in a while; it could be incredibly beneficial in socializing. This may mean thinking about a person you haven't talked to in a few months whom you really miss and visiting them.

Do not put it off when it comes to reuniting with an old friend or family. But, step up. Text or call them. Meaningful conversations are also wonderful ways to deal with loneliness.

- *Get a pet*

Getting pets may help in relieving loneliness for several reasons. A quick snuggle with a dog may raise one's spirit, even for a small period. Everyday dog snuggling may also help the owners' spirits improve and lessen loneliness. A pet is literally a medicine to heal your pain, as research suggests.

Not only can the animal itself give company, but they may also bring up the possibility of meeting new people while taking them out or attending training classes. People are more ready to converse with strangers if a dog accompanies them.

- *Avoid Negative Self-Talk*

The fact that you devote attention to the thoughts you give yourself and the world around you makes the things you think about most often manifest themselves in your life.

You should attempt to recognize these notions and, in their place, tell yourself something uplifting or encouraging. It takes effort and practice, but positive self-talk may be an effective component of a basic treatment for feelings of loneliness.

Suppose you opt to engage in online therapy. In such case, you will obtain an in-depth awareness of the numerous ways for participating in productive internal discussions. It is a powerful approach for warding off negative feelings, and doing so may make a tremendous impact on the quality of your life.

- *Do Something Random to Experience the New Excitement*

You need to get the most out of your hobbies for the feelings of loneliness to stop manifesting. You may prefer watching movies or playing video games alone, but this isn't necessarily the ideal method to cope with loneliness. Find those who you can perform activities with.

Bring forth your best effort to uncover some intriguing and new interests that will put you in contact with others. It might be the impetus you've been seeking when it comes to increasing your social life.

It is time to adopt an alternative approach to operating. Now and again, get out of bed early and take a new route to work. While out and about, check if there are any new creative courses like art or dance that you may join.

- *Create something.*

Do something significant to you such as sketching, knitting, painting, taking pictures etc.

Creative arts have an incredible power to elevate and transcend our unpleasant emotional experiences via self-expression, as well as to connect us more profoundly and truthfully with each other. I usually enjoy writing down my thoughts at the precise moment I feel sad or lonely

You may adopt the act of practicing expressive writing, scribbling down ideas and sentiments you recognize, even if you never share it with a soul. Although, sharing your thoughts might be a healthy approach to finding connections among other people.

You can also express how you're feeling by painting, writing a short story, completing a puzzle, learning a dance routine, or recording a version of that song you can't get out of your brain. Since loneliness might stick around for a while, it helps to have an outlet.

- *Stay Away From Toxic People*

It isn't always a simple task, but there is a need to eliminate toxic individuals in your life since doing so might enhance your mental and physical health. It may not take you long to recognize the individuals in your life who are harmful to your health.

Emotional abuse may arise from dealing with someone who abuse you, mistreat you, or criticize you often. As a result, you may start engaging in self-destructive conduct due to the humiliation or abuse

- *Seek Professional Help*

Sometimes we need the help of health care professionals or therapist to escape the negative thoughts keeping us in solitude.

Long- term loneliness can lead to depression. The more isolated you are, the sadder you get,

In certain circumstances, going out and meeting people is not enough. Even while you're in their company, you may still feel alone, which might suggest sadness or social anxiety. Psychotherapy may be a good alternative if this is the case for you, particularly if you are also suffering other symptoms of depression.

CBT, in particular, may help you to modify your beliefs and behaviors so that you not only feel less lonely but also have more skills to prevent it from occurring. You should do whatever it takes to lessen your feelings of solitude and remind yourself that you're not the only one.

- *Check your social media use.*

Social media use may have both beneficial and harmful impacts on individual life.

While we may use social media to build important relationships, spending too much time on it might lead you to retreat in undesirable ways in other areas.

If we feel unsatisfied with our face-to-face connections, we typically escape into the realm of social media, which only exacerbates the situation. On social media, it looks as if everyone else has better jobs, bigger homes, and better relationships than we do which isn't true. If social media is dragging you down, it might be time for a temporary screen detox.

- *Make a schedule for yourself and stick to it.*

You probably have a daily routine of getting up, eating, working and exercising, but maybe your life needs a little more structure.

Feelings of loneliness frequently seem like they'll continue forever and there's nothing you can do to escape the gloomy cloud hovering over your head, but that's not true. You just need to start making new plans for yourself.

You hardly think about your lonely state, when you have a goal and a purpose. So, set alarms for an early-morning workout or meditation, a phone conversation with your friends or family member, an evening dance class etc. Pre-planning them will fill you with a feeling of control, too.

Once you've come up with a schedule, adhere to it as much as you can. It'll be challenging sometimes, but as long as you take it one day at a time, the planned pattern will seem more and more natural.

Helping people to deal with loneliness

It can be really difficult for anyone to admit they are feeling lonely and it can be even harder to ask for help. And in todays busy world, we get so caught up in our day to day lives that we forget about connecting with those who are important in our lives. It is important to reach out to people who are lonely, so that they know they are not alone. Helping others to deal with loneliness includes;

i. *Reaching out*

Just being there for them and letting them know you are there and that you care may be quite beneficial. Don't be scared to ask them how they're feeling, having someone to listen may be a huge consolation. You can send a message, call them on the phone, or go for a visit.

ii.   *Let them talk while you listen*

It may be hard to listen to someone who is lonely as the conversations tends to be negative at times but let them express themselves freely and then move the conversation to something lighter or positive. This lets them know that you've heard them and that you respect them for feeling comfortable enough to open up.

iii.   *Help them to feel comfortable initially.*

Do not try to force them into the activity that you feel would be beneficial for them. They could require a warm-up time beforehand. For example, let us suppose you have a friend who has been extremely lonely and you want to try and get them to go back out there on the tennis court because you know how much they used to love playing tennis.

Instead of attempting to get them to start playing tennis cold-turkey after a few years of not, you may start by asking them to watch tennis on TV with you a few times. Then you guys could simply play together for a time. And only then, introduce the notion of scheduling local tennis matches. In other words, most individuals will need to ease out of loneliness rather than suddenly breaking free of it.

iv.   Focus on quality time rather than actions.

Let's assume you've got an older parent who is very lonely and you want to assist. So you resolve that you will make a point to contact them frequently. Rather than believing that your talks are a type of mission where it is your responsibility to find out why they're lonely or come up with strategies to assist them to feel less lonely, instead simply concentrate on being there with them. You don't have to speak about anything in particular or even be extremely helpful. Often, simply being there with someone whos lonely is by far the most beneficial thing you can do.

v.   Encourage them to try new things or make plans to do digital fun things with them

Encouraging and reassuring a lonely person that attempting new things is good can be helpful. You can provide additional support for them in accessing the necessary information, like a timetable of local activities. You can also check on them to know how it went.

Make plans to do something fun with them digitally; it gives them something to look forward to. There are fun ways to socialize online including; virtual exercises, virtual book clubs, game nights, virtual exercises, cooking classes etc.

vi.   Be clear about your feelings for them.

This is one of those things we all presumably know but need to be reminded of. Even though the lonely individual understands that you care about them, they may not feel it. This means one of the most useful things you can do is, to be honest about how you feel about that person: Say words like I love you; remind them of what you truly like about them; tell them explicitly how your connection has been essential or valuable to you.

 A lot of individuals who feel lonely are unwilling to be emotionally expressive, even if they know they should. You doing so may convey a signal to them that it's alright to do so and hence make it a bit simpler for them to follow suit.

vii.   *Being patient and encourage them to reach out when feeling down*

When someone is lonely, especially if their loneliness is connected with poor mental or physical health, they may be impatient or feel misunderstood. Patience and gentle reassurance may go a long way in helping them and showing them care. Also, the importance of reaching out when we are in need of connection cant be overemphasized. Letting your friend know you are on the other side or only a call away even if its only online or video chats can be really helpful.

viii.   *Be persistent (but not aggressive)*

If someone you care about has battled with loneliness for a long period, that's unlikely to improve quickly. When you're trying to be supportive of lonely individuals: it could appear like they're not appreciative or making any effort, but in fact, it might be that there's more movement occurring than you can see and that you simply need to be patient. On the other hand, you don't want to be forceful or aggressive.

Why Feeling Lonely Can Get Worse with Time

When lonely, we tend to feel cynical and skeptical of others. This is because deep down in our nature, loneliness is connected with feelings of rejection and danger.

Even when you decide that you want to be left alone, you still feel that society is rejecting you, and the mental distance between you and other people increases with time, if you don't do anything to stop it.

This may worsen the feelings of loneliness through the following means

You cease connecting to regular people since you spend a lot of time on your own, which makes it much tougher to start establishing friendship.

You start losing your social abilities. Social intelligence is like any other sort of intelligence if you don't exercise it, you lose it.

You grow irritable: When lonely, challenges and disappointments tend to look greater to deal with

You lose some of your motivation: A little mingling may give you all the vitality you need after long periods of working hard while the absence of it might make working towards your goals matter less.

The fact is, loneliness drains our energy and makes our goals and dreams appear much harder to reach. So its better to take quick and meaningful steps to deal with it.

Chapter 3

Loneliness in Relationships

Loneliness is not a feeling reserved for the single or lonely ones. It can also happen to those who are in a relationship. Having a partner you spend time with the most doesnt mean you won't be lonely; it doesn't also solve the problem of loneliness. It may be surprising to realize that many people end up feeling lonely in a relationship as well.

Feelings of loneliness in relationship can mean different things for different people. It can mean feeling unheard or not listened to by your partner, feeling unloved or not cared for. Loneliness can also occur when one person look to their partner to fill a void that they have been carrying inside them for long.

Loneliness in relationships can start when the other person feels that their presence or absence has little effect on their partner. A person can also feel lonely when their partner is physically present but mentally absent. If two people cannot talk to each other about their feelings, fears, worries or vulnerabilities, they may feel lonely in a relationship

People can be lonely in a relationship when something isnt working in the relationship. This can happen when the emotional connection is no longer there.

There are going to be times when one or both partners may have drifted apart and feel estranged from one another even in the best of relationships.

In the relationship I had with my ex, I have never felt lonelier than when we are not getting on together. I enjoy the company and love we share but I could also feel the connection slipping away. I could sense us breaking away from that which ties us so tenderly together. I tried to find solace in my solitary space thereby shutting down and alienating myself from others . . . and this is how loneliness begins

Shutting down in relationships never works.

I have come to recognize that when I shut down it is an effort to protect myself from getting hurt more, and it is also an attempt to attract attention from others.

Is it normal to feel lonely in a relationship?

Feelings of loneliness may come to everyone and at any time in their life, in or out of a relationship. Its relatively common to sometimes feel lonely in a relationship whether you are long distance or you live together. Disconnection can happen even if you are in a healthy relationship because sometimes life has a way of pulling us apart. But that doesn't mean loneliness in a relationship is necessarily normal. If you feel alone in a relationship, its often a sign that there is an underlying issue in the relationship or in your personal life that needs to be addressed

Loneliness in relationships doesn't always mean you should break up. You just need to have a talk with your partner and work together to tackle it.

Indications of loneliness in a relationship

Loneliness is a sensation of feeling lonely, alienated and disengaged from others. Signs of loneliness in a relationship can be different for individuals since our experience of loneliness varies and its also individual-specific. Below are few signs of loneliness in a relationship:

- You don't see each other often or long for each other anymore

- Isolation, or less desire to spend time with your partner

- A change in communication. You no longer have deep conversations or eager to share stories about your everyday life

- Neglecting or not completing daily responsibilities

- A desire for more physical closeness with your partner

- You feel the coldness in your relationship even when you spend time together.

- Changes in your eating pattern and health

- You start having different interests

*Ongoing emotions of separation and disengagement from your spouse may be the clue that you are in a lonely relationship

Why do some people feel sad and lonely in their relationships?

Relationships are different, and so are reasons for feeling lonely and unhappy in a relationship which is unique to individuals situation. It can be confusing to feel sad and alone in a relationship. And even when you are able to identify the feelings you are having, it can be difficult to understand what made you feel this way. Factors for loneliness in a relationship include:

- *Distance and physical separation:*

When a partner is gone for long periods whether due to military duty or job, it can lead to feeling sad and upset, the physical separation may lead to one or both parties suffering with loneliness.it often take time and work to build a strong and healthy relationship and distance can stand in the way of that.

- *Lack or Loss of intimacy*

A lack of intimacy can often make you feel undesirable or make you worry about what your significant other feels for you which may lead to feelings of jealousy and insecurity over time. Also,

Some relationships simply lose their spark. If you experience a lack of connection and love, you may be left merely going through the motions. Intimacy plays a huge factor in being deeply involved. Without this connection to your spouse, you may begin to experience a sense of isolation and separation, which may lead to feelings of loneliness

- *Lack of communication*

Some relationships lack good communication. When you do communicate, it might be about superficial things and will likely not have much depth. If you aren't communicating with your partner, you may feel lonely.

- *Incompatibility*:

There are times when the initial thrill of a new relationship gets replaced by the realization that both of you are just not compatible .Couples who get together and finally realize this may wind up in a dead-end relationship.

Resentment, intolerance, impatience, and misery may replace what was previously a joyful life. If you find yourself in a relationship like this, loneliness might be among the emotions and sentiments that rise to the surface.

- *Lack of shared interests*

When partners do not share a common interest, it may lead to one partner attending events and activities alone. Over time, this may result in you drifting apart and spending less time together. This can lead to feeling like you don't share your whole life with your partner.

- *Health problem*

Feelings of loneliness may develop in relationships when a partner is struggling with a chronic illness, facing a major condition, or spending time in the hospital.

You may feel stressed, anxious and lonely. Apart from the need to support your partner, you may also need support yourself. There are also times you will miss the support and companionship of your partner. This can cause an isolating experience.

- *Emotional issues or mental health problems*

Issues like drug use and depression may create loneliness in a relationship. Problems such as alcoholism and other addictions can be self-isolating and lead to loneliness. It is important to involve a health care professional, therapist, or counselor to address the underlying problems including the causes and effects.

- *Physical or emotional abuse*

Any sort of abuse, whether physical or emotional abuse in a relationship may undoubtedly lead to loneliness. This can lead the abused partner to emotionally distance themselves from their abusive partner. It can also lead to depression, drug use, and injuries, as well. If there is abuse happening now or in the past, please speak to your health care practitioner or a therapist about it.

- *Vulnerability reluctance*

An unwillingness to be vulnerable may also lead to feelings of loneliness in a romantic relationship. One contributing factor to loneliness is not talking about your feelings or sharing things that are maybe a little less safe and risky to share. You might be close to someone, yet they might not know the more intimate facts about you.

- *Social media*

Social media might also play a role, comparing your relationship to the ones you see on social media might induce a feeling of loneliness. When you compare your relationship to others on your social media, you may end up creating an uncomfortable barrier between you and your spouse. It is through this distance that feelings of loneliness start to emerge. And the more time you spend on social media, the lonelier you might feel.

- *Existing loneliness in a partner*

Occasionally, feeling lonely might precede the actual relationship. Entering into a relationship as a method of alleviating pre-existing emotions of loneliness would never completely help. People aspire for this other person to be the answer to their existential aloneness in the world, but typically that's not the case. There is not this individual who going to take away that alone-ness.

How can you overcome feeling lonely in a relationship?

It's extremely frequent that individuals find themselves in long-term partnerships feeling lonely; People in a relationship might be lonely because something isn't working in the relationship or other reasons. Whatever the cause, here, are few ways to address the source of the loneliness you may be experiencing.

- *Have a chat with your partner*

If loneliness arises from your relationship and you're expecting to get back on track, it is necessary to have a chat with your spouse. Talking to your partner might be a difficult thing to do but since your partner cannot read your mind to know your thoughts and feelings, it is necessary. The very first thing to do is to become self-aware of what you are experiencing and then to contact your spouse and begin what will probably be a series of dialogues, that should happen in a manner that your partner doesn't feel judged. Let your partner know what your experience is and how you feel. You and your partner may be able to work together for the betterment of the relationship.

Suggestions for easier talk are;

*Pick a moment where neither of you are too tired and irritable and when you won't be interrupted

*share what you what you are feeling, making sure your spouse doesn't feel criticized or defensive?

It is vital to start from a position of vulnerability when you're describing how you feel and to use a non-accusatory tone and vocabulary. For example, you may say something like, I want to trust you with what's occurring in my inner world, I've been feeling somewhat neglected lately, and I don't want you to hear this as blame, but simply my experience. Tackle this as if you and your partner are on the same team and the loneliness is the problem to be solved

*Consider also admitting any pressures your spouse may have in their life that might be limiting them from truly being there for you.

*Don't be afraid of being vulnerable with your partner. It can be hard to bear our soul sometimes, but it can bring the connection we need

*Then, listen to your partner's point of view. If they are on the same page about wanting to restore the relationship, you may conduct a series of talks

targeted at finding out what may be broken in your relationship and how to fix it

- *Don't expect your partner to meet all your needs*

While your partner may meet some of your needs, you should make sure that you have other outlets to feel fulfilled in the relationship. It is asking too much of anyone to expect that another human can fulfill or meet all our needs. You may be putting too much on your partner if: you only ask help from your partner, you always need your partner's opinion on everything or when you don't spend time with anyone else.

- *Explore intimacy with your partner*

The Lack of intimacy can bring a sense of loneliness for both partners. Couples may find it hard to be physically intimate when they are not feeling emotionally connected. Few ways to explore intimacy includes:

* Taking time to say I love you

* Take time to write note a note to your partner

* Take time to arrange a weekend escape or a romantic night.

* Even a stroll in the park together might help reduce a sensation of loneliness.

* Carve out even a tiny portion of time to concentrate attention on each other

* Do chores that you don't normally do together

* Explore new sexual positions or touch other than sexual touch

* Take time to show appreciation and respect for each other

- *Spend time with your friends*

Spend some time among friends or family: That you feel lonely in your relationship doesn't always imply you feel lonely when you're with friends or loved ones. Spending time with friends allows you to have different experiences and opinions shared which can give you greater feelings of contentment.

If the companionship of others helps soothe your lonely relationship, then make arrangements to do activities with others. For example, you can invite them to your house, go out for lunch, spend time working at the gym together, connect after work or watch movies together

See whether these moments of closeness might help lessen your feelings of loneliness with your partner or spouse.

- *Talk to a couples counselor*

Sometimes, loneliness can stem from deeper issues, such as abandonment or attachment issues. It is important to talk to a therapist to address these issues and not wait until things get worse to do so. There is no shame in asking for help. In fact an outside perspective could be just what you need.

Some therapy time with a couples counselor may assist you and your spouse in discussing what might be leading to loneliness in the relationship or marriage. A therapist can even advise strategies to move through it.

- *Find a hobby or Get active outside your relationship*

At times, People tend to lose themselves and forget that they are separate individuals in a relationship.

Maybe spending less time with your spouse or partner might help reduce the feelings of loneliness and enhance the connection.

You should identify what activities you used to do and see if you still enjoy it. Figure out what makes you happy, take time to do things you enjoy whether it's singing, dancing, painting, as doing these things will keep you feeling refreshed or rejuvenated.

Also, volunteer options, hobby clubs, jogging, bicycling, and gym groups, are all viable methods to direct your efforts elsewhere and add satisfaction to your life, beyond the confines of your relationship

- *Take a break from social media*

Social media can help connect individuals, but it can also contribute to feelings of loneliness, especially for people with low self-esteem. The continuous viewing of other peoples life on social media can often lead people to think that others have more interesting or social lives. However, this can compound the feelings of loneliness.

- *Invest in yourself and practice self-care*

Get to know yourself, take time to learn about how you thrive as a person. Explore self-help books that have an effect or impact on you and can help you grow.

Also practice self-care attitudes that can make you happy such as; getting a massage, spending time to exercise, taking a long bath, listening to your favorite music, getting your hair and nails done, reading a book, going to the gym etc.

Chapter 4

Can you be happy alone?

Do you like being alone? Does living a lonely life have to make you unhappy? Is there a way to live a lonely life happily? Research does imply that society regards singles as being deviant, particularly women. Still, if you are happy alone, you are probably self-confident enough that negative perceptions just dont affect you. Also, living alone can serve its purpose: it helps us pursue individual freedom, self-reflection or realization, self-focus and personal control. You get to do what you want, when you want, on your terms.

There's a difference between being lonely and being alone. The main difference between being lonely and being alone is the emotional attachment you feel. Loneliness is a sensation or feeling, being alone is a state of being. Loneliness has to do with the connection with oneself.

Some bask in solitude but for others, being alone is a challenge. You may be entirely pleased being alone and extremely unhappy being among a gathering of people. Sometimes individuals feel lonely while they're in large groups, among family and friends, or even in marriages.

Some individuals are naturally happy alone and prefer to be alone. They enjoy their own company-, and that's natural. They are confident in themselves and are happiest when they are on their own, enjoying their hobbies. They wish to live alone and/or work alone. This doesn't imply they're unhappy, lonely, friendless, loveless or antisocial. That's simply being alone, not being lonely.

The difficulty of being alone only comes when you start to develop emotions of loneliness. It is like you're missing out on what everyone else is doing. Sometimes you may even sense FOMO (fear of missing out). If you spend a lot of time on social media, you may have a case of FOMO that creates a greater sense of loneliness.

Some require a balance of alone time and time spent with other people in social interactions.

Do you feel lonely, or do you love solitude? If you prefer being by yourself but you start to feel lonely, what can you do to alter that?

If you're feeling lonely, consider seeking out social encounters. Maybe get together with a friend or a small group of friends in some quiet place where you can converse.

Regardless of how you feel about being alone, building a good relationship with yourself is a worthy investment

While you are happy or comfortable being alone:

Take Care of Yourself

It's vital to recognize when you need time alone and when you need to be with other people. Being lonely and happy doesn't have to be tough. The more familiar you are with being alone the more prepared you are to cope with feeling lonely.

To take care of yourself and your mental health, you need to know yourself and your emotional requirements. Taking care of your physical health may help boost your overall happiness. Its also a good way to foster a good relationship with yourself.

Try to make regular exercise, getting enough sleep and eating a balanced diet part of what you do with your alone time.

Sometimes you need to recharge in your area. Going out with people is nice, and working with people is terrific, but not everyone thrives in such environments. It is crucial to recognize your boundaries and to know what provides you delight.

Self-love

Self-love is one way to live a lonely happy life. It allows you to reach a new level of happiness and security. When you choose not to go out, it's hard not to feel like something is wrong with you. Being introverted is fine it doesn't mean you don't love being around other people. You derive your energy from being alone, and that's entirely ok. The crucial thing is that you love yourself, even when you're alone.

You need to know yourself to love yourself. If you understand what you need, you'll be more likely to be pleased if you're alone. Loving yourself comes first before you can love anybody else. At the end of the day, we're all alone in our ways. It's vital to love yourself and who you are.

If you're satisfied being alone, you have a healthy connection with yourself. We all need a mix of being alone by ourselves and being with other people. If you're lonely in a group of people, you may need to evaluate your relationship with yourself as well as others to understand why you feel lonely in a group.

Ways to Fill Your Time in a Meaningful Way

You may be lonely and happy at the same time if you do activities to keep yourself engaged, both physically and intellectually.

Mindfulness practice, hobbies, physical exercise, cooking, baking, and reading are all means to be alone and happy. If you're feeling lonely, go for a quick stroll. Do something that helps you feel connected to yourself.

Another way that individuals demonstrate being happy alone is by traveling by themselves. Traveling alone may help you discover things about yourself that you wouldn't necessarily know if you were with another person. You can have good experiences that can change loneliness into happiness.

There are various ways to be lonely and happy and occupy your time in a meaningful way:

➤ Develop a healthy relationship with yourself

> Maintain positive habits

> Learn something new or do things that ignite your passion

> Leave some room to challenge yourself

> Spend time in nature

> Make plans for your future (where do you want to be both personally and professionally in 10 years)

> Practice gratitude

> Take a break from social media

> Take yourself on a date

> Volunteer

> Meditate

> Adopt a pet

They may seem small but these are things you may do in your day-to-day life that might help you to feel pleased to be lonely or happy alone.

Whether you live alone by choice or you just haven't found the right partner, it is absolutely possible to live a fulfilling life.

Living in Solitude

Solitude is often mistaken for loneliness. It is common for people to think that solitude only refers to time spent extremely alone, such as a week locked in a remote cabin.

Solitude is a state of being - it is the state of being alone without being lonely. Loneliness on the other hand, is a negative state, marked by a sense of isolation where one feels as if something is missing. Solitude is a positive and constructive state of engagement with oneself.

Also, living in solitude can be for positive or negative reasons. For example, there are some people who spend time alone because they like quiet or privacy, and there are some who spend time alone because they usually do not enjoy spending time with others.

However, the implications of long-term social isolation can be distressing. It includes depression, poor health outcomes, and early death. This is particularly true when people don't want to be alone, like in the instance of solitary confinement or the isolation encountered by many elderly adults

But what about individuals who, for purpose of adventure, tranquility, spiritual quest, or plain preference, choose solitude? While the great majority of us need social stimulation and a network of support, few have chosen, and allegedly profited from, a life of reclusiveness.

Solitude is more enjoyable if we chose it and we feel good about spending time alone which means we are in control of it. Also, solitude can be beneficial to us only if we can regulate our emotions effectively and maintain positive relationships outside of it

People who pursue solitude of their volition give report of feeling full of ideas, thoughts or things to do. Solitude can have a calming effect on our minds and bodies which can be refreshing and restorative. And when silence is involved, it can help to lower stress, improve sleep and help decision making in some people.

Being comfortable with solitude is the ability to experience our feelings and thoughts in their strong, natural or rawest forms. However solitude can appear to be overwhelming for some people who may struggle to occupy their time or find it tough to be alone with their own thoughts

The upshot is that, while solitude may have many benefits including physical, emotional and spiritual benefits when chosen, spending too much time alone can affect the mind and body. We function best when there's a balance- when spending healthy time alone, and at the same time nurturing our close relationships.

Why do some individuals choose to retreat from social interaction?

1. Inner Peace

Inner peace means mentally and spiritually at peace by freeing your mind from worry and negative thoughts. Many individuals who have intentionally chosen solitude have done so to obtain a feeling of rest and calm, finding quiet itself to have healing or restorative effects.

2. The Hum of the Natural World

Some people enjoy a relationship with nature that makes them feel less alone because of its aesthetic attributes. Viewing a sunset, waking up slowly listening to the birds sing, walking in the forest, being surrounded by mountains or flowers, listening to the ocean waves while sitting at the beach can be sheer bliss. Nature touches the senses of humans and inspires their inner essence.

3. The Spiritual World

Some favor alone time, finding it far more calming and gratifying than human contact and the major purpose in the choice of their hermitage is a religious one. A hermit is a person who desires to live alone, who does it with the purpose of, in some way, discovering God.

Historically, monks, nuns and other clergy members or acknowledged spiritual leaders have occasionally lived in seclusion to concentrate fully on their goal of oneness with and worship of the divine.

Other reasons for solitude includes:

- Solitude increases productivity. People perform better when they have a little privacy

- Some prefer solitude because they feel uncomfortable, anxious or can't be themselves around others

- Solitude sparks creativity. Being alone with your thoughts gives your brain a chance to wander, which can help you become more creative

- Some prefer solitude because they don't feel liked when with others

- Space to breathe. Solitude can be divine for those trying to escape or break the cycle of busyness in their lives

- Being alone can help you build mental strength. People who enjoy alone time experience less depression. This gives better life satisfaction and improved stress management

- Being alone gives some the opportunity to plan or rediscover their life. Quiet space provides an opportunity to think about their goals, progress and changes they want to make in life.

- Solitude provides time for self-examination, self-discovery and reflection. Solitude helps you know yourself or stay in touch with your feelings.

Conclusion

Loneliness is a common emotion that many of us face at times, whether you lack companionship in your everyday life, feel left out and without a connection to people around you, or you've moved across the country away from family and friends.

No matter the reasons why you are personally battling with loneliness, realize that many individuals have experienced the same issue. You are far from alone. Loneliness affects individuals of all ages, in what some health professionals regard as a rising pandemic. Somewhere between one-third and one-half of Americans feel lonely always or sometimes

When we're feeling lonely, we imagine that everyone else has more fascinating things going on in their life than we have. Whether this is true or not, we tell ourselves that we shouldn't bother them.

The last thing we want is for somebody to spend time with us out of sympathy. So instead of reaching out and inviting someone over for dinner or a glass of wine, we hide behind pride and make ourselves lonelier.

It is easy to believe other people have these wonderful lifestyles and are too busy for us. Most of the time is simply not the case.

However, loneliness is a condition that can be fought against and conquered. We believe it shows weakness, but it doesn't.

This is one of the greatest reasons we suffer in silence from depression, from loneliness, from everything that life throws at us that we should be able to handle. We appear to need to struggle on through feeling down, and a lot of us would prefer to go on in quiet sorrow than face the shame of revealing it to another person.

The reality is you don't need a right to be lonely. It may happen at any point in your life. Whether you're young, old, you've recently had a kid, or whether you're in college surrounded by others, you might still feel alone.

It might be uncomfortable to admit that you feel like you have no friends since it makes you seem pathetic. (You're not!) And neither is it something to be embarrassed about.

To admit it might make you feel weak and undeserving at the moment, but the fact is it will make you stronger. Admitting that you're going through a terrible period is strength, not a weakness

Why not attempt to reach out to others to build new connections? You may join a group or class you're interested in or volunteer in your local community. If this sounds too overwhelming, you may prefer to join an online group instead.

If you have friends and relatives that you connect with often, consider speaking up to them about how you feel. Let them know you're battling loneliness. If you've experienced the loss of a relationship, a loved one, lost a job, relocated to a new area, or experienced other circumstances that have separated you, let them know how they may be able to assist you to feel less lonely.

But if you're not comfortable with this, try and build new relationships with others and open yourself to them.

Take the time to additionally check in with yourself and how you're feeling. Ask yourself how you're sleeping and eating, as well as how your mental health is. Take time to build new contacts and reinforce existing ones, whether that's online or in person.

Try talking to a counselor or therapist. They may help you go through the issues that may be contributing to it, recommend extra ways to fight loneliness, and alternative treatments, and help you establish coping skills that work for you.

Everyone passes through gloomy moments in life loneliness being among them but you will find a way to survive and reestablish important relationships.

While living alone or being isolated is simply one of many variables that contribute to feelings of loneliness, when it comes down to it, it is how you feel that counts, not the number of close friends or loved ones in your life. And since lonely individuals are at a greater risk for numerous physical and mental health conditions, including depression, knowing what might cause loneliness and how to cope with it is vital. The key is to realize how you feel and select the ideal technique for you.

It is also crucial to remember that at the end of the day, there isn't one specific technique that will work for everyone who is attempting to push past emotions of loneliness.

It might be daunting but you can take your
loneliness into your own hands and make attempts
to manage and finally conquer it.